CAREERS THAT SAVE LIVES

AID WORKER

Louise Spilsbury

W

FRANKLIN WATTS

LONDON • SYDNEY

Franklin Watts
First published in Great Britain in 2016 by The Watts Publishing Group

Credits
Series Editors: Sarah Eason and Jennifer Sanderson
Series Designer: Emma DeBanks

Picture credits: Cover: Shutterstock: American Spirit (bottom), Northfoto (top); Inside: Dreamstime: Antonella865 23, Gillespaire 16–17, Mares Lucian 20–21, Steve Mann 17t, Photographerlondon 22, David Snyder 21r; Shutterstock: American Spirit 7, ChameleonsEye 15, Chris Dorney 2, Charlie Edward 25, Vlad Galenko 4, Sadik Gulec 4–5; 27, A Katz 10–11, Kojoku 18–19, Vasiliy Koval 8r, Sura Nualpradid 26, Snig 27, Tashatuvango 1b, 28, Tracing Tea 9, A. S. Zain 12–13, 14–15, 24.

Every attempt has been made to clear copyright. Should there be any inadvertent omission please apply to the publisher for rectification.

Dewey number: 363.3'48
ISBN: 978 1 4451 4513 6

Printed in China

Franklin Watts
An imprint of
Hachette Children's Group
Part of The Watts Publishing Group
Carmelite House
50 Victoria Embankment
London EC4Y 0DZ

An Hachette UK Company
www.hachette.co.uk

www.franklinwatts.co.uk

URGENT APPEAL

CONTENTS

HELPING PEOPLE

Do you know what job you would like to do when you are older? What matters most to you about the kind of work you might do? People choose their careers for a variety of different reasons. Emergency aid workers want to help people who are in real need all around the world. They work to improve the lives of those who are poor, in danger or in other difficulties in countries **abroad**.

Challenging Careers

Being an emergency aid worker can be challenging, difficult and sometimes dangerous. However, the people who do this job love their work because they get a huge sense of satisfaction from helping others. Emergency aid workers will work for non-government organisations (NGOs), charities and private organisations. These companies and charities, such as OXFAM, the Red Cross and the United Nations High Commission for Refugees (UNHCR), offer services and aid all around the world.

Aid workers help people in different ways, from delivering food to building schools.

Aid workers help people in desperate need all over the world.

A Career for You?

What is the best way to choose the right career? Start by working out the answers to these basic questions:

• What are you good at? What do you like doing? What do other people say you are good at?

• Do you like being outdoors or inside? Do you like to work with people or alone?

• What do you know about the sorts of jobs you might like to do? Reading this book is a good place to start.

HEROES AT HOME AND ABROAD

Aid workers do some of the most worthwhile jobs. They are trained to help people who face life-threatening challenges at home and in countries all over the world. They may travel to dangerous places during and after **natural disasters**, such as floods and earthquakes, to help people who are injured or have no water. They help people to find food and **shelter** when they have had to leave their homes because of war. They help people to get the equipment they need to make a living when they have lost their **livelihoods**.

Doctors use their medical training to become aid workers and treat people who are ill and in need.

WHAT MAKES A GREAT AID WORKER?

Aid workers are trained to do their jobs. However, they face challenging situations that can change overnight. As well as training, aid workers need certain **characteristics** to be able to carry out their job well. Aid workers must be:
- Caring: aid workers put the needs of others before their own.
- Adaptable: they need to be able to adjust to new conditions.
- Quick to learn: when they are placed in a new area with new problems, aid workers have to learn quickly.

Which of the above do you think is most important and why?

Becoming an Aid Worker

Aid workers need to have a university or college degree. The type of work they do may depend on what degree they have. Many aid workers study **sociology** or **economic development**. Medical aid workers need a medical degree. Competition for jobs is strong, so people often volunteer first with **charities** or other aid organisations.

IN THE OFFICE

When people think of aid workers, they often think of them travelling to exciting places in faraway countries. This does happen, but the truth is that many aid workers spend a lot of time in offices, either in their home country or abroad.

There are a lot of important decisions that aid workers must make. Aid workers attend meetings to discuss plans, how to apply for or spend money or how to help people. They have to work out budgets for the projects they are working on and write reports about their work for **headquarters**. They also have office meetings with people from the **community** where they work, to find out what people need and how they think the aid worker could best help that community.

Working With Budgets

Different aid workers do different types of work, but many have to create or work with budgets. Budgets are calculations about how much money is needed to do something and how much should be spent on different parts of that job. That is why many aid workers need training or experience with money and computers, to be able to handle budgets well.

People think being an aid worker is all about adventure, but aid workers also have to do a lot of paperwork.

WHAT MAKES A GREAT AID WORKER?

Aid workers need to be patient. It can take a long time to get the funding or help that is needed to make projects work. How do you think being patient can help aid workers to deal with the months, or even years, of office-based work it can take to get a **development** project started?

DISASTER RELIEF

Aid workers help people in all kinds of disaster situations. They help people who have been injured, or have no food or shelter because of floods, earthquakes and hurricanes. When a disaster hits an area, especially in a developing country, many people are affected and help is needed immediately.

Taking the Lead

Some aid workers do not hand out food parcels or aid directly. They organise **volunteers** to do this work. For example, they organise the delivery of food supplies, the trucks necessary to deliver that food and the volunteers to drive those trucks to where they are needed. They make sure those volunteers know exactly where to go and how to distribute the aid when they arrive there.

When aid workers arrive at the site of a disaster, their first job is to quickly work out what needs to be done most urgently. Some aid workers give medical treatment to injured people. Other aid workers **distribute** emergency supplies, such as blankets, clothing, food and water. Some try to help those who have been separated from their families to find their loved ones.

It takes a lot of organisation to make sure aid is fairly shared and distributed to where it is most needed.

WHAT MAKES A GREAT AID WORKER?

In a disaster situation, aid workers have to work closely with other emergency departments, such as firefighters and police officers. They also deal with local staff who work for other aid agencies and volunteers from the local community. How do you think being a good team player, someone who works well with others, helps aid workers to do a good job?

MEDICAL AID

All over the world, there are aid workers who are trained doctors and nurses. They deliver medical assistance to people who need it quickly.

Medical aid workers run **clinics** in developing areas of the world. These clinics mean that people can drop in without having to pay anything and get treatment for themselves or their families. Medical aid workers also carry out **vaccinations** to stop people from getting dangerous diseases. After a disaster, medical aid workers travel to the affected area and set up **temporary** hospitals, with beds and equipment, so they can start treating the wounded immediately. Medical aid workers may also work in **war zones**, treating injured soldiers from both sides of the battle.

By giving this baby a vaccination, the aid worker will save him from catching a life-threatening disease in the future.

WHAT MAKES A GREAT MEDICAL AID WORKER?

Medical aid workers have to be adaptable. When working abroad they may have to **diagnose** and treat medical conditions not often found where they live. They may have to work without the equipment they have at home. How do you think being able to adjust to new conditions quickly can help medical aid workers to do their job?

Medical Training

People must be fully qualified as doctors, nurses or **specialists** in particular diseases before they can become medical aid workers. Most aid agencies and charities also require aid workers to have been working in a hospital or clinic for at least six months within the two-year period before they start their job. This ensures that the medical aid workers are up to date with modern medical methods.

DISASTER PREPARATION

Little can be done to prevent natural disasters, but aid workers can train people to be better prepared if they do happen.

Some aid workers help communities to organise early warning systems for people in areas of danger. This gives them time to move away from the area before the disaster strikes. Aid workers also build shelters where people can stay during events like hurricanes. Some workers train local people in **first aid**, so they are ready to help people injured in a disaster. This also means people will be ready to help themselves if and when they are faced with another emergency.

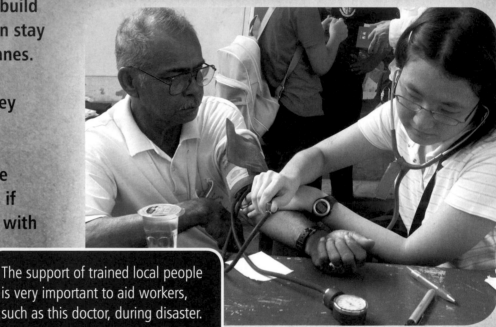

The support of trained local people is very important to aid workers, such as this doctor, during disaster.

Keeping Healthy

Aid workers visit areas where there may be disease, dirty water and other things that can make them ill. It is important that they see a specialist to get **vaccines**, medicines and advice on how to stay safe and healthy while they are travelling. It is also a good idea to visit their own doctor before they leave home, to make sure they are physically fit for the demands of the job. They should also have a check-up when they return.

After a disaster, this aid worker is finding out what people need to help them to prepare for future disasters.

WHAT MAKES A GREAT AID WORKER?

Aid workers often travel far from home and may be away for six months or more at a time. They may stay in places without regular electricity supplies, which means they may not be able to make regular contact with family and friends at home. What **sacrifices** do you think aid workers may have to make in their personal lives?

SANITATION

Clean water is something many of us take for granted, but providing a community with water and sanitation is one of the most important ways to keep people healthy.

Some aid workers teach local people about diseases that can be passed on in dirty water, and the importance of washing their hands. These local people can then return to their communities and teach others about the importance of good sanitation. Some aid workers work with communities to build wells or **water pumps**, to bring supplies of fresh water to a village. This vital work also saves children and others from having to walk miles every day to fetch water.

These people are watching as drilling to create a well takes place in their village. This will provide the villagers with clean water.

Technical Experts

Technical aid workers are trained to do things like work out how much water a community needs. They are also trained to work out where, and how, it is best to drill a well or water pump. They know which materials to use. They are also trained to teach local people how to build the pumps and wells, and how to maintain and mend them.

Aid workers' technical skills and knowledge is vital in helping to complete a sanitation project.

WHAT MAKES A GREAT AID WORKER?

It is important for aid workers to listen to what communities want. Aid workers must find out all they can about an area and its **resources** from local people. For example, local people may know the best place to build a well. How do you think being a good **communicator**, being able to pass on and take in information quickly and clearly, helps an aid worker to achieve the best results?

HELPING REFUGEES

Refugees are people who have had to leave their country, often because of war, and are too afraid to return. Aid workers help refugees in different ways.

When refugees first flee their homes, they may escape to a place where they have no food or shelter. Aid workers deliver tents, blankets, kitchen sets, baby packs and medicines. Refugees may have to live in tents for a long time before they find a new home, so aid workers continue to help them there. Aid workers try to find homes for the refugees in other countries. They also help the refugees to get money or jobs, to help them survive when they first arrive in a new country.

Paperwork

Aid workers must learn how to fill out forms, **applications** and other types of paperwork to be able to ask for financial and other forms of help for refugees. Paperwork is also needed to **reunite** refugees with missing family members, and to help them to find a permanent place to live.

Keeping records of what refugees have and need is a vital part of some aid workers' jobs.

WHAT MAKES A GREAT AID WORKER?

It can be very difficult to organise help for large numbers of people at a refugee camp or for victims of a natural disaster. Things often go wrong or do not go as planned. Aid workers must be determined: they must have a strong feeling that they will get something done, no matter what. How do you think this determination can help aid workers to do their job in difficult situations?

FAMINE RELIEF

Famines happen when a region has an extreme shortage of food. They usually take place in countries where there are **droughts** that cause crops to die and farm animals to starve. These countries are often very poor, so they do not have the money to buy in enough food to feed people during a famine.

When there is no rain, plants die. Without plants to feed themselves or their animals, people go hungry, too.

WHAT MAKES A GREAT AID WORKER?

Aid workers need to be tough. It can be very upsetting seeing people, and especially small children, who are starving to death. Why do you think is it important for aid workers to be both caring but also not overly affected by other people's suffering?

Aid workers provide famine relief in different ways. Some aid workers work in their home countries, where they make up boxes of food supplies to send out to famine-hit areas. Others work out how much food is needed per person and where to send it. Aid workers can fly or drive the food boxes to where they are needed, or help to distribute them. They also treat people, especially children, for malnutrition. This is when people have had so little food they are very ill and may be starving to death.

Deliveries of food are vital when an area is suffering a famine.

With Malnutrition

Aid workers working in famine situations are trained to know when a child has severe malnutrition. These children are very thin because their bodies have used most of their fat and muscle for energy, in order to stay alive. Aid workers must give the children special, high-energy food to help them to get well. They must also give them medicines to treat any **infections**.

DEVELOPMENT PROJECTS

Development projects are those that help people in developing countries to work out long-term solutions to problems. Most people want to be able to care for themselves and their own communities, so aid workers try to find ways of helping them to do this.

Aid workers meet with people to find out how to help them to become **self-sufficient**. They might organise and supply farm equipment to help people to start up farms. They may organise **loans** of money to help people to start up, or rebuild, businesses. Some aid workers train people in new skills, so they are able to deal with future challenges. Others provide materials and teach local people how to build bridges and roads. New bridges and roads make it easier for people to travel, which helps them to find work and to sell the goods they grow or make.

Providing people with useful materials, such as these hoses for irrigation, allows them to build businesses.

Knowing the Area

Aid workers must read about, and spend time in, the place where they are going to be working. This helps them to fully understand how the people there think and behave, and what matters to them. This ensures aid workers can work out long-term plans that will really help local people.

When aid workers organise farm animals for a family, that family can become self-sufficient and may not need to ask for aid again.

WHAT MAKES A GREAT AID WORKER?

Aid workers have to be intelligent and good at research. Before they start a development project, they study different options. They then try out some of the options to see if they work before spending a lot of money on them. How do you think such a thoughtful approach helps aid workers to achieve results that really count?

WORKING WITH CHILDREN

A lot of the work that aid workers do helps children. However, children have particular needs and some aid workers specialise in working with children in need.

Children, like adults, need food, water, family and shelter. Once these basic needs are met, children also need education. When people are poor, live far from schools or have become refugees, children miss out on education. In some areas around the world, aid workers help to set up schools and teach there, or they train adults to be teachers. Some aid workers train older children with skills that will give them a better chance of getting a job. Children also need to play. Some aid workers, for example, in refugee camps, run centres where children can come to play. This helps them to forget the troubled world outside for a while.

At schools, aid workers can give children an education and food.

WHAT MAKES A GREAT AID WORKER?

Aid workers have to be **empathetic**. They need to be able to understand what people are going through to be able to persuade them to accept help. Sometimes, some parents refuse to send their children to school because they need them to earn money for the family. How can being empathetic help aid workers to make parents understand the importance of an education for their children?

Aid workers can help children who have lost their parents and have to look after their brothers or sisters by themselves.

Street Children

Some aid workers are trained to help street children. These are children who have no homes and live on the streets. The training gives aid workers the skills to gain the trust of these children, so that they will accept help and food. The aid workers may also find the children a new home and family.

RISKS AND REWARDS

Aid workers face some risks. They may work in war zones or countries where there are natural disasters. They also work in places where there are diseases, health threats, such as dirty water, or insects that pass on diseases. Most aid workers may face discomfort. For example, they may have to live without electricity or hot and cold running water. However, aid workers are trained to care for themselves and others in these difficult, and sometimes dangerous, conditions.

Aid workers have to consider the downsides of the job before accepting it. However, most believe that the rewards are worth the sacrifices. Most aid workers say that living and working in different countries can be fascinating and very exciting. Many say that on a good day, when things go right and they make someone's world a better place to live, it can be the best job in the world!

Aid workers help to put smiles on the faces of children in need.

WHAT MAKES A GREAT AID WORKER?

A great aid worker is **dedicated** to the job. Aid workers give 100 per cent effort to the job they do, because it can mean the difference between life and death. Could you have the dedication it takes to be an aid worker?

Long Hours

Aid work is not a nine-to-five job. Aid workers are often expected to work long hours for no extra pay. They must be willing to work during their free time to learn more about the area where they are working, or to research ways of helping the community they are with.

Aid workers often work in difficult conditions to help people in need.

COULD YOU HAVE A CAREER AS AN AID WORKER?

Do you want to become an aid worker? Following these steps will help you to reach your goal.

Subjects to study at school
You do not need to study particular subjects, but you need to be informed about the world. Geography, economics, religion and sociology might be helpful subjects to take.

Work experience Volunteer with charities and aid agencies at the weekend and during school holidays. Later on, do voluntary work at home or abroad to gain experience. Aid work is a difficult and important job, so most charities and aid agencies prefer to hire people who have experience before sending them into challenging situations.

Qualifications You will most likely need to have a degree, and some people also get a master's degree that relates to aid work. The type of degree you get depends on the type of aid work you want to do. For example, if you want to do medical aid work, you will need to get a degree in medicine or nursing.

Build your knowledge Learn about aid work through books, articles and websites. Learn about the different kinds of aid work that people do and what organisations employ aid workers. Make sure you are healthy and fit, and take a first aid course, too, if you can.

Getting the job Aid work is very competitive, so you will need to have something special to make you stand out. If you apply for a job with an aid agency, make sure the experience you have gained is suitable for them.

GLOSSARY

abroad In a foreign country.

applications Formal or official requests to someone who is in charge of something you want or need.

characteristics Features or qualities belonging to a particular person or thing.

charities Non-profit-making organisations set up to help people in need.

clinics Places where people can go to get medical treatment or advice.

communicator Someone who is good at giving and receiving information.

community A group of people living in the same place or who share a common interest.

dedicated Devoted and completely committed to something.

development Improving something.

diagnose To work out what is wrong with someone who is ill.

distribute To give out.

droughts Long periods of time when there is little or no rain.

economic development Making a community richer.

empathetic Having the ability to understand how another person feels.

famines Situations in which many people do not have enough food to eat.

first aid Help given to a sick or injured person until full medical treatment is available.

headquarters Places where the people who control organisations work.

infections Diseases caused by germs.

livelihoods Ways of earning money to live.

loans Money that is borrowed.

natural disasters Disasters caused by nature.

refugees People who have had to leave their country and are too afraid to go back.

resources Things that are useful.

reunite To be joined with something or someone again.

sacrifices Giving up things that you want to keep.

sanitation The process of keeping places free from dirt.

self-sufficient Able to live without help or support from others.

shelter A structure, such as a house or tent, which protects people and things.

sociology The study of society (how people live and work together).

specialists People who have special knowledge and training to do a particular job.

temporary Lasting for only a limited period of time.

vaccinations Putting vaccines into the body, usually by injection.

vaccines Substances that protect against particular diseases.

volunteers People who work without being paid.

war zones Places where battles are being fought.

water pumps Devices for getting water from under the ground.

FURTHER READING

Hamid's Story (Seeking Refuge) Andy Glynne, Wayland Books

Immigrants and Refugees (Mapping Global Issues)
Cath Senker, Franklin Watts

Refugees (Global Issues) Cath Senker, Wayland

Stories About Surviving Natural Disasters (Real Life Heroes)
Jen Green, Franklin Watts

Support Worker (What We Do) James Nixon, Franklin Watts

WEBSITES

Find out about the British Red Cross and the work they do during natural disasters at:
www.redcross.org.uk

Find out more about aid workers and the UN at:
www.un.org/en/sections/what-we-do/deliver-humanitarian-aid/index.html

Find out about the work of Oxfam at:
www.oxfam.org.uk

Find out more about the role of an aid worker at:
https://targetjobs.co.uk/careers-advice/job-descriptions/277133-aid-workerhumanitarian-worker-job-description

Note to parents and teachers
Every effort has been made by the Publisher to ensure that these websites contain no inappropriate or offensive material. However, because of the nature of the Internet, it is impossible to guarantee that the contents of these sites will not be altered. We strongly advise that Internet access is supervised by a responsible adult.

INDEX